Morning Letters

❧ MARY'S MESSAGES OF HOPE AND LOVE ❧

JENNIFER COOMBS

Dedication

I dedicate this book with love to my mother, Indira Aslan, and father, Walter Coombs (in Spirit), who have each supported me in countless ways on my spiritual journey.

Blessing to the Reader

Live without fear: your Creator has made you holy, has always protected you, and loves you as a mother. Go in peace to follow the good road, and may God's blessing be with you always.

(Quote from Saint Clare of Assisi)

Acknowledgements of Gratitude
to the Following

Christen McCormack, founder of Spirit School, for her unparalleled gift of connecting with and guiding others in the dimension of Spirit. She has taught and inspired me for several decades.

Paolo Coppini, creator of the original painting of Mother Mary, for his generosity of spirit and absolute mastery and artistry.

Jo-Ann Langseth, my editor, who, as she most accurately states, edits with "near-papal infallibility." I was guided to her by Spirit and she has brought another level of beauty to Mary's message.

Kirsten Perry of Kirsten Perry Designs, for her artistry and responsiveness in bringing the dimension of Spirit to all interior artwork and the book cover.

Kemper Conwell of Pixels, for her highly intuitive and proficient editorial and publishing assistance.

Introduction

My conscious journey with Mother Mary began a number of years ago as I began to turn to her for guidance about my family. I remember feeling, and seeing reflected in the questions I posed, a great deal of timidity in approaching Mary with my concerns and worries. But now as I reread her messages, it's clear that the wisdom and loving support she imparted has stood the test of time, and bears witness to the invaluable love, comfort, and inspiration that Mary can provide.

Three to four years ago, I began to receive messages intuitively that I was to be a channel for Mary to bring a book about love into the world. It took a great deal of courage to finally share this with someone who could validate this intuitive guidance. At that time and for a number of years thereafter, I could not conceive of being worthy enough to work with Mary on this undertaking.

The actual writing of the first part of Mary's book began in the late summer of 2014, as ISIS began its very public and horrific executions of journalists. It was heartbreaking beyond description, and precipitated my turning to Mary on a regular basis as a lifeline. In addition, I suffered a number of losses over the next several months that shook the foundation of my life.

Yet this book is not about my personal losses, struggles, and fears. Suffering is part of human existence, and all humans must pass through many trials and tribulations throughout their lives. I feel blessed not to have experienced the depth of loss and suffering that many in this world have had to endure. Mary wishes to use my struggles and questions as a kind of base from which all who seek it may find comfort and hope. Her compassion and counsel remind us that all of us face similar struggles, challenges, and losses at different points in our lives.

The times we are living in are challenging to the extreme. Many dark forces are abroad that threaten life as we have known it. Great instability has arisen in many governments and institutions. The generally secure financial structures that previously existed in the lives of many can no longer be counted on. This book is intended as a source of support through these upheavals. Life will continue in this pattern of more and more extreme challenges and shifts for the next three to four years. During this time we are called upon to serve as beacons of light and love for humanity and the Earth. Mary and all other beings in Spirit who tend to us wish to support us through this transition in all ways possible.

Through these writings, Mary also wishes to extend her gift of unconditional love to all who are open to receiving it. Connecting and communing with Mary has given me my first real feeling and understanding of what it means to be loved unconditionally. She has tirelessly counseled me, offering wisdom and loving support. Without exception, Mary has led me back to hope whenever I fell into despair. I was frequently directed to reconnect with the things that I treasure in life – children, nature, and beauty. She has taught me that I am always worthy of being helped. The blessing that she extends at the end of our time together is real – and beyond description. I know these blessings have transformed my being and my life.

It is my hope that this book will be of help to you in passing through your personal challenges as well as those we are experiencing on the planetary level. It is also my wish that through these pages, you may experience the resplendent and unconditional love that is offered freely to each of us, if only we will summon the courage to ask for help. I have been reminded time and again that Spirit is unendingly generous.

Blessings to all!

October 4, 2014

Mary,
My heart is broken by another public beheading.
My heart aches for the great suffering and agony that is
being inflicted on innocent people.

My Dear,

This is the great tribulation that I spoke of. Earth is in one of its darkest hours. You are being held in the embrace of the Comforter during these hours of suffering. You will not be forsaken during this period of personal and planetary grieving. When you find yourself in despair, as you do now, call upon the Holy Comforter to envelop you in its embrace. Call upon its deeply loving and healing support for others in need of its Presence. You are a light unto the world, especially during these darkened days.

Yes, forces must gather together now in great number to defeat this force that has lost all connection with Light. That is only the beginning, though, of the profound changes that must come about on Earth. Some, at least, are beginning to recognize this. You are being asked to serve as a vehicle for drawing others close to the Presence of Peace. That is the energy, the vibrational reality, of the Master.

Go in Peace, my dear. You are being held in the unending embrace of the Holy Spirit.

Mary

OCTOBER 26, 2014

Good morning, my dear,

We wish for people to understand that, in these most troubling and even frightening of times, the Source of hope, courage, healing, compassion, and forgiveness is available to any and all who call upon it. This Source, God's Love, is accessible to all who appeal to it with an open heart and mind. Let me clarify that further and state that even the *willingness* to call upon the Source with an open mind and heart will suffice. Faith is built upon these moments of willingness.

All of you are witness to many acts of violence being committed against fellow human beings. You are witness as well to the conditions of work becoming more and more dehumanized. Fear of illness and death arise easily in the consciousness of mankind from the outbreak of Ebola. The deafening din of life in a speeded-up pace of living seems to almost obliterate the symphony of silence playing underneath.

Yet it is during these most troubling of times that you are called upon to activate the Source of Love in the Life of Earth. Your role is essential, and your work with Spirit is indispensable to the healing of the hearts and minds of mankind and to the healing of Mother Earth.

Rest now. We will return to take up this teaching again in the near future.

My blessings,
Mary

Good morning, my Dear One,

Let us gather together to speak of Love again, using your own personal example. You have sadness in your heart this morning from an uncomfortable exchange at work yesterday. Honor this feeling, it will pass fairly quickly, and it is food for transformation. You were witness to a lack of empathy and normal human caring that flows from Love. Your sensitivity to the energy of others allows you to feel the reality beneath the words and expressions that convey messages not in alignment with the truth of the moment.

Detach, if you can, so you can observe the false self in action. The false self, without a connection to the Light and Love of the soul, is capable of great harm. Without any grounding to the Source of Goodness that lies within, the false self is interested only in gathering more to itself — more power, more glory, more accolades, and more specialness. The list is endless.

You looked to this person's reactions in your conversation, noticing the evident lack of empathy, and made the mistake of thinking she chose to be self-absorbed. You believed she consciously chose not to extend empathy. Understand where her center of gravity is, send her well wishes for turning toward the Light, and understand that you are not present to a person not choosing Love. The false self chooses only itself. It is incapable of loving.

The work with the false self must be taken up with commitment, though it doesn't have to be onerous. With the attention brought back to Love and Light – that are the true nature of the soul – you simply step aside from this complex that makes up the false self, over and over again. This is a process that will go on in most people for a much extended period of time. It is easier for most to have the false self disengaged slowly over time as a new, more real self begins to emerge. Remember, all starts with clear seeing and intention.

Use these instances of mankind's forgetfulness and failure to reside in their own Light – including your own – as a reminder of the need to return to Love over and over again.

My blessings,
Mary

My Dear,

You must not think that you cannot turn to me when you are ensnared by low feelings. You are not unworthy because you are struggling with sadness, fear, or anger. These lie within the realm of human emotions. Your feelings of unworthiness stem from a mistaken judging of these emotional states. This is a time when I can be of greatest help to you.

The emotions that arise within you are truly wonderful guideposts to deeply held beliefs and ways of seeing yourself and Life, all calling out to be seen and known. There are often layers of truth that need to be illuminated and understood. Understanding leads to liberation. Do not be ashamed of your feelings of sadness, loss, or vulnerability. They are the warp and the woof in the tapestry of your life. Each has a beauty of its own, though it may not be your favorite color or pattern.

This is so important to understand. Healing cannot take place without it. Embrace your child that is sad and frightened in the same way you would your own precious daughter or son. Remember that I am here at all times to support and comfort you in your periods of struggle and loss.

With Love,
Mary

November 7, 2014

My Dear One,

Your heart is heavy today, especially with the loss of your friend. You are feeling as well the grieving of many others who are strongly connected in Spirit at this time through the loss of one in your circle. His loss will be felt for some time to come, and his passing will accelerate the growth and understanding of all connected to him.

This aching of your heart is one of the beautiful yet painful experiences of earthly Love. It is made even more painful by the circumstances of his passing. Yet it is in these moments of grief that you are brought to a purity of heart, and dwell in the sacredness of the Eternal Now.

There is nowhere to turn to escape the wellsprings of sadness that seem to have no bottom. Yet this grief rolls in like a tide, stays for some determined length of time, and then, in alignment with the nature of life, it again recedes.

Life will never be quite the same again, and yet this tear in the life fabric of so many will be knitted back together in a unique way – different for each. The healing of broken hearts and shattered lives will be a testament to the healing power of God's Love for each of you.

In the days to come, for as long as you need, honor him with beauty, with humor, and with Love through nurturance and patience for all things. Let this significant event in the lives of many be a great reminder to you of the preciousness of Life, and that Life itself is an unfathomable mystery.

Be in Peace, my dear. Know that you are loved unconditionally, just as you are.

With my blessings,
Mary

November 13, 2014

My Dear,

You weep for your losses this morning. They are real, and it has taken some weeks for their impact to make itself known. Know that we in Spirit stand right by your side. You shall not have to endure these trials by yourself. We are available at a moment's notice to give you solace, hope, and the vision of a new direction. In those times when a comforting friend or family member is not available to you, we are here. You are being cradled during your times of grief. Allow your tears to flow – this is a natural and necessary part of the process of letting go. It takes courage to stand alone in these times, and all of mankind face them at one time or another.

Underneath the sorrow is the Peace of God. This is the salve for the wounds you have endured during this period of multiple losses. When the Presence of Peace makes itself known to you, as it did this morning in the midst of your tears, proclaim your choice for joy, for happiness. You create an opening for them to arise, to take you by surprise, for events to unfold that lead to the unfolding of your dreams.

Reconnect with nature as often as possible – even if it sets off a stream of tears again. Eventually, with the passage of time, acceptance will arise. Life will give birth to new work, to new deeply satisfying friendships, and to new love in many forms.

There are many in the world who have suffered great losses. Let this be a time of tenderly caring for yourself and extending yourself to care for others, whenever possible. Rest in the knowledge that you are deeply loved and cared for. I am here with you.

My love,
Mary

November 17, 2014

Mother Mary,
I need help with how to handle all the evenings
I am alone now. I don't want to turn to my usual,
unhealthy patterns to deal with my loneliness.

Yes, My Dear,

Loneliness, feelings of loss, and feeling at a loss as
to how to bring feelings of connection and joy into your
life plague most people at one time or another. You are
looking for feelings of connection to fill your evenings, and
you are turning to a source which never fails to disappoint
you. Your children were and still are a great source of
sweetness for you, but they are grown now and their
absence leaves a hole in your life. The safety and comfort of
being held within the embrace of love is the sweetness your

heart longs for. You have that in a number of places in your life, but long to have it present in a more profound way.

Let us in Spirit guide new friends and families to you. Your work is to visualize the meaningful connections that you desire. Visualize the gatherings in your home, the outings to visit and spend time with new, dear friends, and the bringing of gifts to celebrate life's events and life itself.

Life is endlessly creative, and when your heart's desire is in alignment with what God desires for you and for others, then Heaven and Earth will move to bring it into manifestation.

I am always here to help.

My blessings to you,
Mary

November 19, 2014

Good morning, my Dear One,

Your heart is troubled again this morning by pangs of loneliness and fears of isolation. Know that this is only temporary. Your longing to have sweet connections in your daily life is nothing to hide or be ashamed of. It is an arena of your life that needs loving attention and healing. Your fear of not being chosen has often deterred you from taking the courageous steps needed to build loving, deeply satisfying friendships.

You must choose new friends carefully. You have the model of very dear, old friends who unfortunately can no longer be in your daily life. You wonder at times why friendships have not manifested in different circumstances, and you have looked to yourself as the cause. Timing is sometimes part of the reason, but most often it is a disharmony in energy or level of being. You are looking for a safe place to share yourself and open to receive the beauty and wonder of another. This is becoming increasingly rare among people at this point in earth's evolution. Rare, but it definitely exists.

Again, I remind you to turn to me and others in Spirit with prayers for help in bringing these beautiful connections into your life. You must move past your deeply held belief that your needs are not important enough to trouble others with. Think of how deeply satisfying it is to help your families and children in CASA. They too have difficulties with believing they are worthy of being helped.

Reflect on the visible signs of healing that shine from their faces as they take small steps into a sense of their worthiness. That gives you some sense of what we in Spirit experience as you do the same. Hold this vision in your heart so that you do not hesitate to call upon me or others. Your sense of unworthiness does not serve you or others in any way.

My deep love to you,
Mary

Mother Mary,
I have one whom I love very dearly
whose anger from a betrayal is consuming her.
Can you speak to this?

From Mary

This has come as a disguised blessing, but she is as yet unable to recognize it as such. The sacred healing that her soul desires is to know in a profound way, with unshakeable certainty, that she is worthy of being loved. She looks outside herself for confirmation that she is lovable, and because she carries within her a strong seed of doubt, she chooses those who will set off this inner conflict. The outer world always reflects the inner world.

It is important here for her to step aside from the anger so she may come to sit with her inner child, who is terrified and consumed with sadness. A child not chosen, not attended to with loving care, will wither and perish. Sitting with her child self with the utmost of tenderness and attention will begin the process of healing for her. The anger only masks the almost unbearable vulnerability she experiences when facing this question of whether she is worthy of being loved and chosen.

There is great potential for a life-altering healing at this time. Her heart, which is tender, is aching to blossom into the fullness she knows exists on a deep level. Let her bring all the wisdom, compassion, and deep love she has as a mother and grandmother to the task of unconditionally loving and caring for her own dearest one within.

My blessings to her,
Mary

DECEMBER 22, 2014

Dearest Mary,
It is so difficult and painful to see the suffering of the children
and families I work with. I try to bring the love, attention,
and nurturing I can to their situations, but they have such
a difficult road in front of them.

From Mary:

Yes, the paths their souls have chosen, along which
to both learn and unlearn, are filled with strife at this
point in their lives. You are not able to see the full picture
at this time and so it fills your heart with sadness, and at
times a sense of hopelessness. You must remember that
even though the outward appearance is sometimes bleak,
there exists a spark of the glory of God at the core of each
child, and parent as well. They are not separate from that,
though particularly with some of the parents, that spark is
often clouded over and forgotten.

The souls of these children that you love so dearly
chose this path of separation and abandonment in order
to return to a state of wholeness. Some of these parents
will be able to heal alongside their children. They are all in
God's hands and your job is to hold out the Light of Divine
Presence to them – and to hold it out again and again
because it is so easy to fall into a state of forgetfulness.
Look to your own healing that has taken place to remind
yourself of the reality of the miracle of healing.

Bring the Presence of Love and Joy to each of your
visits. You can count on your compassionate nature to

nurture and be sensitive to the suffering that may be present, but joy and love need to be modeled.

Go in Peace, my daughter. You are serving well, and all will be well.

With love,
Mary

My Mary,
I am beginning to perceive the oneness that is the deeper
reality of life here on Earth – especially in connection with
time and space, and it calms a part of me in a way that I
haven't experienced before. Could you speak more of this?

Yes, my dear,

The Life that lies beneath what you normally
experience as life is so vast and mysterious that it can
barely be spoken of. The oneness that you have begun
to perceive is but a glimpse into the unknowable mystery
that underlies, gives birth to, and supports all of life as you
know it. Through this, all is connected.

The separation that arises constantly in the minds
of humanity gives birth to the myriad forms of suffering
that exist on Earth. It is that simple. You have turned
your attention recently to the sense of isolation that arises
instantly when the mind begins to judge. The mind, the
mind of the ego, erroneously believes it safer to judge and
condemn. In truth, it has condemned itself to detachment
and separation from the nurturing support of connection
to self, others, and the natural world.

The oneness that is common to all things is vastly
larger than your mind can encompass at this time, but
your approach is correct. In those moments when you first
observe judgment arising, step aside from this illusory
form of protection and recall with as much vividness as
possible that judgments are completely unnecessary in

life – that in fact, they prevent you from experiencing true Life, and of course real Love. With keenness of observation and practice, the habitual states of mind, wherein one judges and believes oneself to be separate and alienated from life, will begin to collapse in on themselves. Their unreality will take care of that.

Then the sacredness of Life, that is always and everywhere present, will reveal itself to you. It is waiting for you, for you and all others. It is waiting for the true attention and love that will spring from each. It is what is needed for real communion and a sharing of the oneness that is Life.

This is where we will end today, my dear. My thanks to you for your participation.

Blessings,
Mary

DECEMBER 27, 2014

Good morning, dear Mary,

I had such disturbing dreams last night – of war breaking out here (in the Tyson's area of Virginia, where I first heard of 9/11), of being separated from my children during this crisis, of how close many parts of the world are to conflict and war. Can you speak to this?

My dear,

This is one of the purposes of our work together – to make available to others a source of comfort and courage in these truly troubling times. The Earth is in upheaval at this time to which we are all witness. This will take another three to four years to play itself out and, as you can see, it is taking its toll on many, in many different ways. My heart goes out to those who have suffered great losses already.

There are so many different forces at work here – many are beyond the understanding of mankind in general. A new consciousness is trying to emerge here on Earth, but there is much density and baseness in the consciousness of a great number of people. For these people, many more lifetimes are needed for their evolvement to a significantly higher level of consciousness.

For some of these people, additional resources must be made available so that they may move beyond their pressing preoccupation with survival. As people are able to manifest decency in their living conditions, they are granted the opportunity to address higher-level needs.

Others have satisfied their basic survival needs but are still content to live at life's lowest levels – physically, emotionally, and spiritually. Through the conditioning of family, education, and culture, they learned to go through life with hearts and minds that are closed. Their stasis is difficult, as there is a whole world out there that will support this choice unless they commit to fanning the flames of inner truth and love on a daily basis. This work must be taken up by each soul – it is an arduous journey and there is no guarantee that one will embrace this challenge in any one particular lifetime.

Each can help in their own world. There are many in need whose sense of hopelessness and despair will be lightened when others turn in love to give their support. The presence of hope in one's life is a very powerful force. It is an essential dynamic in creating a new and more light-filled life.

The other essential way you can help is to model a mode of living that reflects an inner life illumined by Love and Truth. Tend to your thoughts, your speech, and actions. You will make a difference, but it is not up to you as to who will follow. Be the Light and Love of the One True Reality of this world.

My blessings to you, dear one. May you be filled with the Peace of the Master.

Mary

Good morning, Mary.

Good morning, my dear,

We speak this morning of judgment – to a larger and fuller understanding of judgment. You have seen into the workings of this process that is peculiar to the human mind. What arises in the mind takes on a reality all its own. One feels obliged or compelled to participate in the process. The fact is, this creation of the egoic mind has no basis in truth. It will instantly crumble or dissolve back to dust if pierced with the arrow of loving awareness. And this is as it should be.

You have observed how the mind of the ego erects walls around itself at the slightest threat. And it does this, without a moment's hesitation, through the automatic mechanism of judging. In so doing, a sense of separation sets in – separation from another person, from an event, but especially from oneself, and from any higher influences that work within you and within life.

There is no judgment here or condemnation of this process. There is only my effort to clarify and illuminate this mechanism that takes place in all humans. I do so, so that you can step aside from this habit that closes the heart and mind to the wonders of life.

Whenever you feel a tightening in your being, in your body, you are receiving a signal to bring the light of your awareness to the goings-on of your mind. Lay

down whatever you are holding against another, aga.
yourself, or against what is arising in the moment. Yes, i
a moment you will feel a bit naked, but this is an invitation
to step into what is alive, fresh, and innocent in that
moment. Herein lies your true safety.

Your safety also provides a safe haven for others.
Your energy field will instantaneously reflect the laying
down of guardedness or attack. The light of your
awareness, whose true nature is love, is given permission
to radiate out again. Its nature is healing – to self and
others. When unimpeded in its expression, it is healing
to the Earth as well.

Intention and effort are all that are being asked of you
to topple the domination of the judging mind and allow for
the natural flowering of the heart. My best wishes to you
in this courageous endeavor.

With blessings,
Mary

Good morning, Mary,
Can you speak today on the rise of fundamentalism in
Islam? Twelve people were murdered in France this week at
the satirical paper, Charlie Hebdo.

Good morning, my dear,

We take up our discussion again about the frightening levels of violence that are arising out of misunderstanding and a lack of love and empathy for one another. The world responds to attack with a show of might. Of course, the perpetrators of violence against a group they feel is a threat to their core beliefs must not be allowed to operate this way in your world. But retaliation in kind with violence shall never bring about a peaceful resolution to their differences, will never bring about a state wherein differing ways of understanding, of experiencing, and expressing life can be allowed to peacefully coexist. This aspect necessary to the healing of humanity and Earth is given very little attention and even fewer resources. The majority of mankind is still invested in imposing their supposed solution through a show and imposition of might.

Fortunately, there are some groups whose work is focused on fostering greater understanding between different religious groups, but the size and number of these groups must increase in order to have a greater influence on the minds and hearts of a significantly larger number of people.

On the most basic level, fear is driving all conflict – and of course it is deeply unconscious. When one sees another who is different from oneself – perhaps in dress, in language, in customs, in beliefs (particularly those that define one's sense of reality, such as religion) – one has a tendency to draw back, to separate oneself from them. One's sense of humanity dims more and more the greater one's retreat into a sense of separation. It takes a more mature spirit to see and acknowledge differences and commonalities in the "other," and become curious about the seeming "stranger." This open curiosity is the beginning of forging a connection with others that eventually, with great dedication, leads to the experience of Oneness.

This work must be performed on many levels in the world, including, of course, the psychological level. You who are called to the Light must dedicate yourselves to this work with great determination fueled by love. There will be many, for some time to come, whose spirits are heavy and for whom darkness is the veil through which they perceive life. Those who can are asked to increase their efforts to cast a light in the world for all who are unable to hold their light at this time.

Organizations that work to foster greater understanding between different cultures and religions should be applauded and supported. It is not necessary to be completely involved with such organizations in order to support them. It is the same with making a donation to a charity – small amounts in large enough numbers make a difference.

The world is moving rapidly to a critical point of change. The incendiary words or actions of a person or group never justify retaliatory violence, but the deeper issue of taking responsibility for the effects of one's speech and actions on others is vital to the future of this planet. One cannot live in isolation and with disregard to the wellbeing of their fellow man or Mother Earth.

Talk among yourselves and see where each of you can make a difference in this regard. Be gentle in the way you embrace each other in your awareness. That will give you an opening to connection and eventually lead to a sense of Oneness.

I continue to send my blessings, especially to all those involved in these conflicts. A great healing is needed.

With love,
Mary

Good morning, my Mary.

Good morning, my attentive student,

You wish for me to speak of addictions, which plague you in no small measure. It is true, as I have said several times in my talks, that all can be healed. That may seem impossible as you look around at the events transpiring daily in life – horrific in some cases. And yet it is as true "out there" as it is in your own inner universe.

All eventually will be healed by coming into the Light, as all that exists in darkness – and can only exist in darkness – is consumed by the Light, and is consumed by Love, which is the nature of Light.

How may this be applied to your world and your struggles with mood-altering substances, such as caffeine and alcohol? At times, you mistakenly perceive the mystery contained in each moment as perhaps emptiness, devoid of meaning or passion, and you retreat from it in fear. By nature, you tend to retreat by chemically altering your mood and state. You have made great strides in staying present to the richness and sense of magic that is contained in many moments throughout your day, but you struggle with times of transition especially. This is not unusual for many.

Can you use music in those times when you wish to retreat as a means to reconnect with yourself? For that is what is missing. In truth, you are looking to reestablish connection with true passion. You are familiar with this essential quality of living and experience it in healthful ways many times throughout the day. Your soul longs for and is fed by experiences of genuine passion and the sense of wonder arising from them.

Think on these things. You chide yourself and feel defeated when you let yourself down, but with intelligent thought, this pattern can be replaced by a thing of great good. We have full confidence in your ability to transmute your "Ugly Duckling" into the Pure White Swan that you are.

Blessings and Godspeed on this journey!
Mary

JANUARY 25, 2015

Good morning, my Mary,
There has been another killing of a journalist – this time a
Japanese man. I cannot allow myself to read about it because
it will affect me so deeply. How will people go about
addressing and correcting the huge issue of growing terrorism
in the world right now?

My Dear,

These events bring great heaviness to the hearts of those in Spirit, especially those tending to the care and evolution of mankind. In some respects, a passage of time is necessary for those who have wielded and are abusing power to see that they will not be able to create and sustain what they imagined would be possible through their abuses of will. There will be many more slayings of innocents, and for this my heart weeps. In time, the minds and hearts of humanity will fill with a sense of this great loss. This sadness will permeate the consciousness of many, most importantly those in a position to bring about change. It is unfortunate, but the horrific events that are going on will have to affect more people in a more personal way before the tide of change can gather the necessary force to bring about true, enlightened growth.

At this time, there is little being done other than the retaliation of warfare. While it is true that these forces of darkness and evil must be stopped in their tracks, it is much more important to address the underlying causes of why so many young people, particularly men, are so willing to take up the cause of these terrorist groups. There have always been and will continue to be (at least for the foreseeable future) those who wish to seize and abuse power. But the number of young people who willingly join forces with them is almost unprecedented. They are not being conscripted; nor do they join out of fear of reprisal. Most join with knowledge of the philosophy and methods of warfare of the group they give allegiance to.

Many factors are at play here, but it is particularly important to address the alienation and feelings of disempowerment that run rampant through the throngs of young people who join forces with these masterminds of destruction. Their plight must be understood, especially by those in a position to effect changes that bring about real transformation.

The thinking that is prevalent in the world today, as it has been for many thousands of years, is very limited in its depth and breadth. It is always about "success," or the attainment of one's goals at the expense or the defeat or failure of others. You see this in the terrorist groups, but you also see it in groups or organizations that have been sanctified – such as churches, governments, corporations, and organized sports. As long as those wielding power in these various groups continue to put their own interests above those of others, this alienation and sense of separation will continue to grow.

Look around, my children, and you will see so many examples in both your personal life and in the life of the world today. The age of the Internet has provided greater transparency for these events, but also calls for greater discernment in its righteous use.

I ask all those of you who can hear this message not to turn away from the sufferings you receive news of nearly every day. Send your light and prayers to those who are enduring almost more than the human spirit can bear. It takes but a few minutes of your time. When others care and make supplications for those in need, it strengthens them in Spirit. It makes a difference. Please join me and others in Spirit who are tending to the needs of humanity, especially those who suffer much at this time.

My love and blessing to you, dear one.
Mary

Good morning, my Mary,
I have reached the end of the security I felt at still having
the pay and benefits of a full-time job. My fears and anxiety
have risen to the surface, especially in my dreams.
Can you speak to me of growing greater trust that
I will be taken care of?

Good morning, my dear,

Yes, you could not have anticipated what this next
level of loss would feel like. As in all of life, the mind
makes a futile attempt to project itself into the future and
create an image of what it thinks a future experience will

be. It falls far short, though, of creating a likeness of what a felt experience will be.

Comfort yourself in as many healthful ways as you can at this time. It will pass, and is another stage in a loss that you have handled with courage and grace. I applaud you for writing this morning, even though your fears have temporarily taken you hostage. Draw close to children, to nature, to animals, and to the comfort of friends and family. They will help you reconnect with that part of yourself that knows the goodness and rightness of life.

Move forward with the steps needed to bring this book and the *Angels Guidebook* to completion. Your new reality needs to be engaged regularly to bring it into manifestation.

I send my blessings to you. Know you will continue to be supported in all ways as we go forward together in this vital work.

Mary

Good morning, my Mary,
I feel sad this morning on Valentine's Day from a spell
of loneliness. I long to have more friendship and feelings
of true connection in my daily life.

Good morning, my dear one,

Yes, I feel the loneliness of your heart this morning. It is a temporary state and will pass, yet it is painful in the moment. You are longing to feel the comfort and sense of belonging that comes with the safe union of kindred souls. Let me reassure you that it is coming – and in fact, with God's speed.

In the meantime, what can you do to create a sense of magic in your life today? Again I remind you to connect with nature in an intimate way. Bring one new thing of beauty, such as a bouquet of flowers, into your home today. Fill your rooms with fragrance and music that inspires you. Feel the joy that begins to fill your being even as you simply visualize doing these things.

This sadness will pass, but assuming the role of co-creator will fill this passage with purpose and feelings of mastery. Let this time be a testament to the power that resides in you to transmute your suffering into a growing sense of trust and safety in the world.

Remember that I am always with you, and stand ready to help.

My blessings to you!
Mary

Good morning, my Mary,
Can you speak this morning of deception, including
self-deception? My attention has been directed to it lately
and I would like a broader understanding of it.

Yes, my dear,

Deception in its many forms is an integral part of life on Earth at this time. You have seen evidence of it recently in your own life, and it is disappointing and hurtful when you find yourself in its path. We will return to talk about better ways to respond and protect yourself a bit later in this letter.

Know that attempts to deceive always come from a misuse of power – either an abuse or an abdication of power. Neither is in alignment with the Source of Goodness and neither leads to results that are satisfying in the true sense of the word, or supportive of life itself. You see examples of both in your life right now and feel the consequences I speak of. While it may be easier to see the destructive effects of abuse of power, the insidious effects of someone abdicating their true power are no less damaging in outcome.

Those who have not yet taken up the work of stepping into and standing in their own power have done themselves and others a great disservice. You are all connected, and the arenas in which you lack empowerment directly affect those with whom you come into contact – whether it's family, friends, neighbors or coworkers. Not taking up your power does not have a neutral effect. Its effects are negative, but perhaps not obviously so at first glance.

You have had plenty of experience with abuse of power in your own life. You have come to know that underneath an exterior that projects strength and force may lie a core of weakness and vulnerability that has never been attended to.

And so deception is used in both cases as a tool to attain what one wants and/or needs. Psychological mechanisms associated with lying are activated to the degree necessary for this process to proceed. Only standing in your truth, being present to your inner life in a loving but detached manner, will afford you a chance to begin to dismantle the network of deception that is harbored by most.

You have seen this taking place personally in the area of fantasizing – in particular, creating visions of a life that would bring greater security, more connections, and communion with loved ones and nature. Your well-developed imagination easily led you into inspired states that seemingly offered answers to your most plaguing difficulties. They took on a reality of their own. Fortunately, you have also been blessed with the dismantling of this particular type of self-deception. It began with taking in the truth of life as it was unfolding in the present moment and being willing to turn to it as your teacher. It has taken courage to be present to the vulnerability you experience with fears and anxiety. Insight into your particular form of flight from life and truth helps you to understand how the process works in others.

It would be best to look dispassionately at the deception to which you are exposed. It is not done with clear consciousness. The mechanisms at work have developed over a lifetime and serve the interests of the false self. Trust in your knowingness that sees who a person is behind the words and actions expressed in the image they project. Trust in that, and remember that people will eventually display their true colors. Steer clear of relationships of all types wherein you find the elements of deception and/or self-deception.

You have experienced new lessons in this, my dear. The effects have been a little painful, but they were mercifully brief. Use this fresh understanding to go forward with greater awareness of safety in the world.

My love and blessings to you,
Mary

Good morning, my Mary,
How do I hold onto faith at this time of additional losses,
and trust that I will be able to discern my path forward?

Good morning, my dear,

Your faith is being tested again, and we in Spirit applaud your willingness to trudge forward down a path you have never taken before. The human mind does not like the insecurity that accompanies this type of passage. And for this reason I extend my gratitude to you for embarking on the next part of this journey, along with your unwanted fellow traveler of uncertainty.

We spoke before of allowing yourself to be filled and supported by the silence that underlies all of life. This morning as you write, a light snow continues to fall. Your world has been transformed again by the singular beauty of a world covered in a blanket of snow. The starkness of the bare tree limbs is made into a thing of beauty by a partial covering of white. And so it is with your life. Certain things have been stripped away, but as with the leaves and foliage, new growth will burst forth when all conditions indicate readiness.

Be present to the stillness and ineffable beauty that underlie and gird these times of apparent loss. Be open to the truth of life as it reveals itself in this moment – not to be analyzed, pinned down, and understood. In so doing, the structures of the mind that are brittle, that cause pain in your daily life, begin to disintegrate. What takes their place is pure, loving awareness. And pure, loving awareness has no need for timetables, or definitive knowledge of where you will live or work.

I am asking much – your losses, though temporary, cause pain. But much is offered in return. An opening into the Sacred, into what is most real and most holy, is the blessing that is extended. You will falter at times on this path – it is to be expected. But a hand will be extended to help steady you again. Stay connected to nature, to beauty, and to children. That will help you to re-establish a connection with your own core of truth and beauty.

Take stock, as you go forward, of all the support and clarity of direction you receive. This will help rebalance the mind's tendency toward negative imagination. And I remind you again, I am always here at a moment's notice to guide and support you. The more frequently you call on me, the stronger the line of connection becomes.

I continue to bless you on this journey.
Mary

Good Morning, dear Mary,
I received notice last night that the agency that oversees
the care of the child I visit has changed its goal from
a return home to adoption. This is heartbreaking
for her birth parents. Can you give me a higher view
and understanding of this?

Yes, my dear,

There is sadness in Spirit that the parents of this beautiful child have not been able to move forward sufficiently in their evolutionary path to rise to their loving duty to the child they brought into this world. It seems likely at this time that this beautiful child will find a permanent home with her foster family. This is a blessed arrangement, and the foster mother is fulfilling a contract she made with the soul of this little girl. Rest assured that all resources will be made available to her and her family in order for them to raise this daughter.

The experiences this child had to endure, including neglect and abandonment, were chosen by her soul to facilitate the healing of her sense of separation and unworthiness. Being seen, loved, and chosen by those in her foster family has significantly shifted the paradigm of her belief systems. There is healing taking place on all levels for her and it will continue to unfold. Her kind and giving nature shall incorporate the losses she has experienced into the essence of what she will give back to the world as she matures. Her losses, untainted by bitterness, will bless her with sensitivity to the pains of others.

It is indeed saddening that her birth mother has not yet been able to get sufficient distance from her own wounding. It is a matter of timing and readiness, but the child cannot afford to wait for her parents to make the critical decision to take up their own healing. The story has yet to play out and will continue to unfold in dramatic and often wondrous ways. There are many lives intertwined here, and each has come together around this child as part of the child's and their own ultimate healing.

God's work is being done here and all are blessed to be a part of it. I send my blessings to this child and all of her family.

Mary

Good morning, my Mary,
I have been ill several times this winter. Can you speak about
illness and disease? I have felt a certain blessing in this
latest tussle with my health.

Good morning, my dear,

Yes, this is a subject of great interest on Earth, and
it is much more multifaceted than you would imagine.
Your latest illness resulted from the cascading effects
of weakened health (due to multiple bouts of sickness)
combined with highly stressful exterior conditions that
were relentless in their effect on you. Your body craved the
deep rest it needed to rebuild and rejuvenate. The spirit
needs a responsive body, a vehicle that is functioning at an
optimum level, to perform the work that it is being asked
to do.

You have been asked to work with Spirit to bring the
Teachings out in the world in a manner that is fresh and
unique to you. This work requires the ability to connect
with and hold a vibrational level that is beyond that
normally experienced in life. It is not possible for you to do
this in any sustained manner when you are in poor health.
This illness came in as a gift and as a strong reminder
from Spirit of the high priority of taking care of yourself.
You cannot be of service to others and to Spirit when your
resources have been so greatly depleted.

During extreme illness, there is a certain purity in
you that can be contacted and invited to manifest more

fully. This only happens, though, when you can manage
to step aside from the fear that so often arises around loss
of health and vitality. The gift that was given was your
contact with the Teachings that came through a book you
had owned for years. The words fell upon your ears and
your heart when you were rooted in greater purity, and
their effect was manifold. "Whoever has ears, let them
hear." Jesus spoke of our becoming like little children,
whose innocence and purity of heart is needed to hear and
understand the Teachings.

In a state of greater purity, new understandings have
the capacity to tear down structures in the ego that are
based on illusion and delusion. And it can happen in one

eternal moment, and without pain and chaos. As it was said, "The truth shall set you free." This was the gift of your illness.

All illness and disease come about through an imbalance, through a disharmony that is calling for attention. You are called to address these as a mother or father would – with unconditional love and wisdom. With extreme illness and disease, the effects on the body may have been too long-lasting to be reversed, but the soul always has a choice as to the path it takes. A person staying in their purity, in their light, serves as a source of lasting inspiration to others.

It is crucial to remember not to impose judgment on self or others in regard to illness. This cross to bear can bring about great transformation in one who, while doing all they can to manifest a restoration of health, stands in surrender to the truth of this present moment. They are always whole and ever shall be. You are asked to remember this.

With my love and blessings for health and vigor,
Mary

March 18, 2015

Good morning, my Mary,
I had a discussion recently that under normal circumstances
would have been very uncomfortable for me. In the midst of
it, I felt a flood of clarity flow through me and felt strongly
connected to my own empowerment. Can you speak to this?

Good morning, my dear,

Yes, that was indeed your own power, your own
truth being released into your consciousness. You have
had several shocks recently that have facilitated the
tearing down of some of the psychological structures that
prevented your power from manifesting more fully. The
belief systems you brought into this life from previous
incarnations, and the ones fostered in this lifetime, had
essentially imprisoned the power and freedom that are
your birthrights.

The experience was a wonderful testament to the truth
that you know, with unmistakable certainty, of how to live
in the world in a harmless way when you reside in your
power. The wisdom of the path to be taken during the
discussion came to you in a flash of intuition. It bypassed
thought and because of that, seemed almost miraculous in
nature. You have long struggled with accessing and
trusting your own sense of knowing, and this situation
has demonstrated to you how powerful this resource is
within you.

This is what living in alignment with the Truth is, and
the experience gave you a taste of what you are being drawn

to. The egoic mind tries to project itself toward what it imagines true empowerment will feel like, but is doomed to fail. Living in the Truth and in line with the empowerment that flows from it is of another realm – the egoic mind is incapable of grasping it.

Having that experience of deep clarity and the gentleness that accompanies it has significantly healed your fear of stepping into your power. You have had mistaken notions that confused true power with the attempts of a person abusing power to dominate others.

This experience has been a real blessing. Use it now to model empowerment to others. Use it to demonstrate that power is not separate from Love or from Wisdom. Let your new level of empowerment be fed by a fountain of overflowing joy.

Great blessings to you, my dear one,
Mary

Good morning, my Mary,
Can you give me guidance on a spiritual practice
that will help me to grow in consciousness?

Good morning, my dear,

Yes, it is good to have a definitive practice that one commits to and engages with on a daily basis. In fact, there are several aspects to this that, if attended to with commitment, will facilitate a more rapid growth and deepening of consciousness.

The first is a regular, daily practice of meditation. As you have been taught, it is necessary to quiet the mind and allow for the body to settle and move into a deeper and deeper state of relaxation in preparation for the Presence of Christ arising. Your intention, your invitation, your welcoming the Divine Presence to abide with your soul's light is the essential element needed – and of course, the commitment of a daily practice.

Your consciousness, your cells, the psychological structures that make up the complex of the self that interacts with the world, are changed by contact with these higher vibrational levels. Continued committed practice brings about continuing change and growth in consciousness – and not always in a linear fashion.

You have innumerable opportunities throughout your day to reconnect with the Christ Consciousness – in an instant, if needed. You have been witness to stressful situations being transmuted into events of neutral or positive effect through an invitation to the Light to manifest fully.

You are also asked to develop a practice of prayer that is in alignment with your own heart's cares and concerns. It doesn't have to be highly structured – only consistent. One can choose to do this at one particular time of the

day or participate in this practice at several different times of the day. I use the word *participate* because you are partnering with Spirit when you pray and are a part of the creative process.

Make sure when you pray that you set your intention to join with the higher vibrational level and light of the entity or being you are praying to. Remember, you are praying for the highest good for a particular person or situation. Focusing on this will help you detach with love from any fear you are experiencing around the situation.

Lastly, you are directed to have other daily contact with sources of inspiration that speak directly to your soul. It could come from poetry, intimate communion with nature, music that moves you to a different place within, spiritual texts that inspire new levels of understanding, and many other sources. All of these can serve to shift one out of the usual state of total absorption in the outer world.

Think on these things. Make a commitment to all three on a daily basis and you will see a quickening of the inner life.

My love and blessings to you, dear,
Mary

Mother Mary,
I'm sad and frightened. What can I hold onto
during this time to ease my sadness and anxiety
that stem from being alone and still without a job?

My Daughter,

This is indeed a trial for you, but it shall pass. Be with your period of sadness and grieving. Give yourself little treats that you look forward to – such as dancing. Avoid activities that are too much for you at present to handle emotionally. Continue to prepare your home for sale. Bring flowers into the home to brighten the energy. Play music while you're home – you are currently too isolated.

It took much loss to bring you to the point of discerning this new direction. It took much loss and disappointment. You are being supported by family and friends and many in Spirit. You feel alone, but you are not. Write more frequently. You need fresh insights, inspiration, and guidance on a regular basis.

You are loved and held within my embrace.
Mary

My Dearest Mary,
So many new truths about myself, my approach to life,
and the ways of the world are being revealed to me right now.
The meeting with D, her son, and my sister has shaken
the "globe" of my world. I am setting off to learn to be
a warrior — for our work together and for bringing this book
out into the world. Do you have guidance for me
about this newly perceived journey?

My Dear,

You are in a state of being blessed right now. Your perceptions are a direct intuition of the self-knowledge that is being revealed to you. Things will transpire quickly now. Remain in this state of innocence when asking for and receiving help.

Let your new friend, M, guide you in your efforts to self-publish our book. Let go of that old habit of letting fear of shame prevent you from taking up the mantle being offered. All will begin to flow now toward rapid manifestation. Let your profound sense of knowing guide you. Opportunities will arise which offer chances for evolution. These will be followed and then replaced by fresh opportunities.

Stay close. We travel together now.

With Love from the Highest,
Mary

Mother Mary,

Please guide me in my continuing struggle with finances.
I feel weak to have to ask for help.

My Dear,

Your struggle is in its final stages and yes, you do need some help to make it over the final hurdle. Let yourself be helped in making it over this finish line. You have fought this fight bravely, and there is nothing to be gained by stoically suffering in silence. All help comes from God, and each true heart is glad to be of assistance to another soul.

Our work together will always need to be supported. It is all the handiwork of God. Ask for help and a lifeline will be thrown out.

My blessings to you and all those who step forward to help you.

Mary

SEPTEMBER 5, 2015

My Dearest Mother Mary,
Can you give me guidance on my mother's condition,
what we can expect in terms of recovery, and whether
there is any chance of her moving here?

My Dearest Daughter,

I see your block toward hearing my guidance but it is not needed. Your mother, though frail at this time, is not ready to leave this earth. She has many important lessons to learn and all of her children will be involved in that learning. There will be life-changing lessons for each of you as well.

This time and trial was necessary for her to endure because the shocks were needed to break down the barriers she has maintained that block true love and intimacy. You will barely recognize her around the time she finishes her journey here, and you will feel deep, deep gratitude for the healing power of God's love.

If she is able to travel back East, it will not be until spring. It would be lovely for her to spend her final years with you, but that is still uncertain. She is being tenderly watched over, as is each of her children.

My blessings to you and your family.
Mary

My Mary,
Can you speak of the refugee situation in the world right
now, resulting primarily from the great conflict taking place
in Syria and Iraq?

My Daughter,

This pains those in Spirit, as well as the many caring individuals who bear witness to the suffering of those who have been forced to flee their homes in search of safety and peace. The world will be in this current state of upheaval for a number of years to come – until almost 2020. There will be a significant reordering in societies, sure to displease a good number of people. And yet, this change which is thrust upon your world will be a contributing factor in the opening of mankind's heart and mind. The prejudice harbored toward others of different nationality, culture, faith, and values is always fear-based. One is afraid of the unknown and therefore rejects it in an effort to stay safe.

Witnessing the refugees' suffering touches a deep center of compassion within those whose minds and hearts are open to a great enough degree. The Internet serves as a tool for educating the minds and spirit of mankind, and more exposure to their fellows' suffering will be necessary to keep people from turning away from that which is painful to behold. Many care and yet feel powerless to do anything to help. Though the crisis is happening primarily in Europe, that crisis is also taking place in truth within the family of mankind, and its solution must be sought from that level.

What can you, as an individual, do to help? My suggestion is that you pray and meditate upon this, and see what you are led to do personally. Talk to family members and among friends to see how you can pull together collectively to make a contribution to alleviating this terrible suffering. Send your prayers daily to those caught up in these conflicts. Select an area upon which you can focus your prayers, if that is more helpful to you. We will speak of this again very shortly. There is much to be addressed.

With my deepest love and blessings for Light in your life. Mary

Good morning, my Mary,
The violence from terrorist groups is rapidly increasing.
They have threatened an attack on the Washington, D.C.,
area. My family is having discussions about the eventuality
of an attack. Can you speak to this?

My Dear,

It is frightening, to be sure, and this is one of the
main goals of radical groups – to create an atmosphere
of fear and disorder in the world, to break down and
destroy structures and cultures of a civilization they feel
is antithetical to their belief systems. They are, of course,
deeply ignorant and have no connection to the heart
of Islam.

There will be violence here within your country. All
must be vigilant and be prepared for disruptions and
disasters that are likely in the coming period of two to
three years. Their organization has grown in the way that
only an invasive weed can grow, and continues to grow
in terms of sophistication and support. They are not
destined to be successful, of course, but will challenge the
world in many ways during their reign of terror. There is
no negotiation or resolution of differences possible with
these groups. They have completely lost touch with their
humanity. The firefight that I spoke of to you a year
ago will indeed have to take place. All countries that are
capable will have to join in this battle against these

darkest of forces. There is no other way to restore balance to the world.

The world will go through an additional transformation during this time. It is a time when most will be led (or forced) to reclaim what is most essential in their lives – love, family, and friendship. A spirit of friendliness and generosity, and a deeper connection to nature and beauty, will be nurtured by the challenges of these times. You experienced a deepening of this after 9/11, but the attacks did not continue in the way that is probable over the next several years.

All who have connection with their light are asked to step forward in their daily lives and serve as beacons through this darkening storm now spreading over the earth. Send light into your daily life, into the places you live and work. Send light and prayers for healing to areas and peoples that are under assault. Healing is needed in great measure at this time, and will continue to be needed.

We will write together frequently throughout this time. These words of guidance, comfort, and hope will be especially needed at this juncture in history.

My love to you, dear,
Mary

My Mary,
It is Christmas Eve again and we arrive at yet another
celebration of the birth of your son. Do you have a message
for us during this season?

My dearest daughter,

Remember especially at this time that this event is about the birthing of love and innocence into the world and into your lives. The celebrations, although they may at times lose sight of the season's meaning, contain the kernel of the truth of the meaning of Christmas. The gifts, the music, even the festive lights are all intended to and capable of inspiring the spirit of love and giving. The magic of Christmas is the same magic you experience when love arises anew in your life, when hope rises up again in your life – especially after you had lost your connection with it.

The true nature of each person is love, and so this annual return to love is actually a return to your own true nature. You are only reminded of and drawn back to reclaim what is yours. It is a rekindling of the impulse to give and extend yourself – both to others and to yourself. The very nature of life is ceaseless unfolding and giving.

Let the little stresses that arise during this season serve simply as signposts to areas within your being that need rebalancing and restoration. Do not judge yourself for perceived shortcomings that come to light during this time. Simply note the imbalance and ask for the new understanding that will restore balance. Ask for an abundant blessing of love and joy from Spirit that will help you realign with your true nature of love. We are only too happy to immediately post this gift to you! That is a joyous aspect of the miracle of this season – the clearing away of all that blocks this flow of love to you – and consequently through you – to the world.

Hold on to the true meaning of this very precious time. Do not be disturbed by the season's excesses, but return again and again to the peace, the innocence, and the sweetness of loving connections that lie at their core. Hold on to this vision, for this is what is intended for mankind and for earth in the not-so-distant future.

My blessings of love to each and every one of you.
Mary

My Dearest Mary,
Can you help me to understand how the
purification of the heart comes about? I desire it
perhaps above all else, and I stumble toward it,
but I wish for more guidance and direction.

My Child,

You must do all you can and desire it with all your being, but the key that unlocks the mystery of Love will be a gift. It is not a gift to be earned or anticipated. It will come through Grace at a time when your spirit is prepared to receive it and sufficiently prepared to express it.

Pray for this gift. Let your prayers be the ground for your going out to and your coming in from the world. Let the vision of life, whose breath and heartbeat are Love, continuously realign your life. You will find that this realignment, by itself, will be sufficient to facilitate the unraveling of fear.

Fear, which blinds you to the presence of love in your life, has no real substance. It has no permanent reality. Fear, when pierced with the truth revealed by real understanding, dissolves and disappears. Fear may break down over a period of time, especially when it is woven into the fabric of belief systems that strongly define your consciousness. But, it is also possible for it to break apart and dissolve in an instant. Be open to this form of miraculous healing. Your receptivity creates openings for this to happen with regularity in your life. Eventually you begin to understand the nature of fear itself. Mankind is under its spell, but you can see the potential for humanity's evolution as more and more people move away from subjugation to fear.

Take this prayer for the gift of Love, for the purification of heart, into your life in deep measure. Let it become one with you, as your breath and heartbeat are. As it transforms your life, others are inspired by it, and will have their desire for it awakened. The spirit of Christmas – of Peace, Love, and Joy – can begin to transform the reality of life on earth as we now know it.

Blessings to you, my daughter. Let Love and Peace reign in your heart.

Mary

JANUARY 1, 2016

Good morning, my Mary,
A new year has arisen. Personally, I feel optimistic this
morning. Can you speak about the coming year
in terms of humanity and the earth?

Good morning, my dear,

Yes, this year will see the flowering of a number of blessings for you. It shall also be a flowering for many others – if they are willing to open their hearts and minds, and especially their imaginations, to a new realm of possibilities. This is an idea that I would like to see spreading among as many people as possible – in fact, spreading like a wildfire that cannot be contained.

The consciousness of each person has a particular density to it and this is determined in part by the belief systems it contains and their particular densities. They are largely unseen and therefore you are not familiar with the taste of them. Your beliefs keep you firmly planted where you are, and prevent you from even entertaining the arising of a new, more joy-filled life.

Your notions about lack and limitation color your perceptions of and define what you think is possible for you, for mankind, and for the earth. As one small example, consider the ways you could contribute financially to assisting in the refugee crisis if you didn't always feel strapped. Creative, enlightened solutions ultimately find their way to problems, but would proceed at an astoundingly faster speed if minds and hearts would open to vastly new possibilities – for themselves firstly and then for humanity.

Pick an arena of your life in which you feel lack, an arena where fear often visits. Related situations will come to mind very easily if you allow your mind to be a stage for this little play. Pay close attention to the feeling tone that sets in. You must become very familiar with this (but with a little detachment), for it is a barometer to your inner world and the belief systems that are active. Now let your soul's imagination usher in pictures or visions of a life that would feel more meaningful, that is more joy-filled. You'll hear objections, coming as a litany of all that would get in the way of this manifesting, but don't let that deter you. Look at the presumed blocks and see where

you might need fresh insights, the gift of courage, more creative problem solving, or greater prayer on your behalf. There are so many creative solutions to challenges. Finding solutions brings a sense of empowerment and gratitude, and it often involves making new connections.

This process will keep hope alive and thriving. The carrying of greater light will attract more of the same. Possibilities that found no opportunity for audition before are now free to present themselves. Your naysayer is losing her voice. There is so much goodness available to all – beyond your wildest imaginings. You are the one who, with wisdom and love, must lay down old, outdated beliefs that stand squarely in the way of a stream of goodness that wishes to flow unobstructed into your life.

My love and best wishes for a bountiful year overflowing with blessings.
Mary

About the Artist

Paolo Coppini was born and raised in Florence, Italy. As a child he displayed an early gift for capturing the character of people in sketches he made of customers in his grandfather's wine shop. He began his studies at the Accademia di Belle Arti di Firenze at the age of 20. Immersed in a life that was inseparable from art, he was strongly influenced by the drawing, composition, and painting styles of the masters that surrounded him – da Vinci, Pontormo, del Sarto, and Masaccio. Rembrandt was Paolo's greatest influence, but he was also inspired by Raphael, Titian, and Caravaggio. His interest in portraits drew him to the Flemish artists and he points to the Venetian school as the greatest – especially for portraiture and capturing the essence of life. He moved to the United States in 1984 and began a distinguished career as a portrait painter.

Paolo likes people and is fascinated by their faces and expressions. The very young and the very old are particularly intriguing to him. His experience is that "In the face of the child is the universe–there is the potential for everything; but in a way there is emptiness, because there is no experience. Yet there is the potentiality of the whole universe. It's like an empty vessel that can be [filled] with anything beautiful…With an old person, you see the result–the labors of love, the experience, the accumulation, and many times you see the spirit within… because after going through all the experience and nearing the end of that lifetime, there is a kind of detachment. So it goes full circle."

Paolo continues to paint portraits of clients, both in the US and abroad. He is available for commissioned work and shows special sensitivity in capturing the essence in spiritual and religious works.

Notes on Images

Since childhood, I have felt a mystical connection with nature. On my journey with Mary, she has always counseled me to connect with nature, with children, and with beauty when I fell into despair. It is the path I take most often when I need to find my way back to myself, and to reconnect with the stillness, the holiness that underlies all of life. It is a way to find my way back to hope and to a sense that all is well, though life contains struggle and suffering.

I have included images in the book that evoke for me that sense of Spirit, that quality of innocence and beauty that can only be hinted at through art, through poetry, and other expressions of beauty. The graphic artist, Kirsten Perry, has rendered the images in a more painterly manner to lead the reader to an experience of communion with the munificence of life. It is my hope that these will enhance the experience of connecting with Mary and will serve as a reminder to turn to those things in life that are most holy to you, for healing and sustenance for your soul.

I wish to give credit to the following for their images and artistry:

Rodion Kutsaev *page 6*

Dan Stark *page 8*

Jon Ottosson *page 10*

Mehmet Kavaklioglu *pages 13, 64*

About The Author

Jennifer Coombs is an intuitive who is drawn to service, providing nurturance and healing through words and presence. Her spiritual journey began in the Gurdjieff Work in Washington, D.C., in the early 1970s. She has been a student of the Spirit School of the Intuitive Arts since its inception in 2000. She is a Certified Angel Therapy Practitioner and enjoys guiding and supporting clients on their paths to greater awareness, empowerment and fulfillment.

Jennifer is the mother of two wonderful, grown children. She lives in Fauquier County, Virginia where she enjoys writing, providing intuitive counseling and volunteering with children.

For more information visit: maryscircle.net

Made in the USA
San Bernardino, CA
26 June 2016